salmonpoetry

Publishing Irish & International
Poetry Since 1981

The Poet of Poet Laval

Carolyn L. Tipton

Published in 2019 by
Salmon Poetry
Cliffs of Moher, County Clare, Ireland
Website: www.salmonpoetry.com
Email: info@salmonpoetry.com

ISBN 978-1-912561-49-0

Cover & Title Page Image: "*The Village of Poet Laval, Provence, France*".
"*[StockCube] / Depositphotos.com*".

Cover Design & Typesetting: *Siobhán Hutson*

Printed in Ireland by Sprint Print

Salmon Poetry gratefully acknowledges the support of
The Arts Council / An Chomhairle Ealaíon

for Frank

Contents

Instructions for Travel

Take a compass.
Make sure it's always pointed towards the sun.
Think of a blue day, of us
entering a new town like a river—
    all its rush, then its drifting, its readiness
        to bear away reflections.

Finger the petal in your pocket
taken from my Valentine's bouquet,
each flower a scene we've seen together:
    those cygnets nestled in the hull
        formed by their mother's back & wings—
            a living swan-boat on the Zurichsee;
    the black-and-white of that full moon night
        we were swifts above the Vltava;
    our balcony above Granada, where the swallows
        swirled like petals in an eddy
            in the dropping space between us & the city.
Enter the world's evenings by remembering how
we stood like gods within the Parthenon—
    so high up it could have been Olympus:
        between the columns only rose-tinged clouds;
we celebrated Summer Solstice up in Wengen,
    lit candles as the alpenglow
        burned Breithorn's white peak pink.
Imagine dwelling in that moment of warm wind: the café
    near the Englischer Garten, the afternoon
        of arrival, the trip bright before us.

Or choose the other door, step through
    as if to a blank page. Here,
the bird has not yet landed on the branch.
There is no branch, nor even an outline
    to show what kind of tree is not yet here.
Only the beginnings of a breeze:
let it lift your outstretched fingers, strings
    attached to possibility, to everything
        still unnamed in the garden.

The Poet of Poet Laval

writes prescriptions for sleep, listing
sonorous ingredients whose names
you only have to read before slipping
into a deep canyon descended
by way of rustling poplars, the humming
of bees in oceans of deep-colored lavender, the slap
of the waves of those oceans, and there at the bottom,
dream's diagonal door of light and shadow, the one
you never are aware of passing through.

The poet of Poet Laval
is a useful poet, writes poems
that seed the heart you thought non-arable:
soon, stirrings, presentiments of
the wild and bright; red poppies.

The poet of Poet Laval
does not exist. Poet Laval is a village, very old,
in the north of Provence. Touched by the thought
of a village named after a poet,
I visited Poet Laval and asked after him:
who had he been, and where could I read his poems?
These questions made everyone laugh, until
a kind woman took me aside. "It's like this", she said,
"in Provençal, 'poet' means 'mountain'"! So,

no famous writer of poems ever lived here, no favorite
son who went to Paris and became renowned,
no local troubadour, whose song about a woman's eyes
—though she's been under ground nine hundred years—is still
remembered. Not even one beloved in his time
for his lyrics celebrating big events: the spectacular
grape harvest, the long-delayed completion of the church,
the late birth to the lonely, childless couple.

And so I conjure a poet for this town.
In her poems—no matter what the words describe—
a window opens up: through it, the evening sky
of a summer long ago, its first stars
through the branches, the rhyming
white blossoms, whose breathed-in scent brings back
the sense that anything is possible.
All of it given back. Everything restored.
Just for the moment of reading, of course,
but the spaciousness lingers inside.

Withdrawal and Return

Like a cocoon wrapt round her,
the water of green leaves;
in it, she will sleep the sleep of birds.

Feathers of the moon, drift down upon her.

Look: she's lying curled inside a shell.
You could say, "like the rounded seed
inside the two halves of a fruit". Except,
she doesn't even hear the sound of waves.

Only the wind knows which boat brings the Spring.

The white path of awakening will be slow.
It goes uphill towards the house; the dark earth
is loath to fall away. But all around,
clear voices: blossoms backlit by the sun.
Something will call out on its way up, green
shoot or budding bird; the rising world
will tug the string wrapt round her hand.

The Next Poem

The next poem you'd like to read
would lift you like a large balloon
and waft you high above the vineyards.
Its words would be the colored folds of silk
filled up so full that finally
they become one seamless globe
that floats off, you along with it,
standing in the basket like
Chagall's bride, a bouquet above your head.

Bouquet above, or floating
flower stall arrayed with
all the sweet produce of Spring—
billowing iris-blue, the hyacinth's curve.
Below, the earth: grapevines, then fields
of cows whose black & white
your shadow further patterns as you pass.

Then in the grass, so far below, a woman.
Her life has grown too small for her.
She's come out to the orchard's edge
looking for something like grace, a sign
that her world will open up again.
It could be anything—maybe a bird
veering so fast that the red of his wing-tip
flashes, maybe the sudden sun
escaping from clouds to dazzle
these white blossoms. A falling star
if it were night. It's not though:
when she looks up, she sees *you*.
You are just exactly what she'd hoped to find.

When I Think Of You
I Think of Openings

You're like the leading character
in that play we saw, the chef whose gift
was to know what everyone
most hungered for: the bowl of purple mulberries
that brought Cornelia's childhood back to her;
the Caribbean stew that let Lucien taste home.

Except your gift is deeper than the chef's because
what we're most hungry for isn't always food.
How do you divine what we most need?

When I think of you I think of openings.
The secret unfolding of the lily; the plum tree's tight buds
giving way to blossoming, a profusion
of moist petals. But also the sky
opening to blue. A revelation to the mind
of something new. And, too, the flowering quality
of desire—how gladly a breathed-on ember
flares to fire.

Coaxing Rafaela

"Chocolate!", my friend cajoles. "Champagne!
Picnics!…You can have a dog!…Madrid!"

Rafaela's late. My friend has been expecting her
all week. I've called to get the news:
"Michael & I are trying to tempt her out."

And so I imagine my friend seated, bent over
her huge belly, speaking softly and selectively,
not of pain, despair, or unrequited love, but only
of the sky's blue when the fog has finally lifted.
She constructs a perfect afternoon: sunlit,
secluded spot; the checkered cloth spread out, upon it
olives, tomatoes, goat cheese, French bread, grapes;
a breeze fragrant with possibility, delicate
scent of apple blossoms, white ruffled with pink,
like her skirt, which his hand slides up…this is how
it all began. "Rafaela, it can be
like this. Won't you please come out and join us?"

Anubis

*(For Rafael Alberti,
d. October 28, 1999,
El Puerto de Santa María, Spain)*

Rafael, at the moment when you died,
I was in a small club in New Orleans.
You would've loved it: Spanish dark-
wood walls; a leaf red pressed-tin ceiling;
a patio, lit by a moon just past the full, and
crowded with the large leaves of banana trees
and palms just like your own trees in El Puerto.
The Rebirth Brass Band played: young guys,
exuberant with their new sound, stepping
up & down the room, inside, outside, led
by the sax-man in the second-line parade
of a black jazz funeral. O Rafael,
I was at your wake and didn't even know it!

You once told me the story of Niebla.
You gave the orphaned dog this name
after she came to you out of the mist
one dark November night in '36. Franco
was bombing Madrid, and Niebla's
home and family had been lost. With Neruda,
you were out walking the streets when she appeared.
She led you through your war-time years, companion
at the Front, where you read your poems to the soldiers,
and in the heavy truck, loaded with the Prado's
greatest paintings, which you drove all night to safety,
and later, on the mountain, where you said
her leaping reacquainted you with joy.

El Puerto, between midnight & sunrise. I imagine
another Niebla approaching you out of the dark.
First blackness, then a black dog manifesting.
The suddenness & red glint of a hummingbird.
Quick look of invitation, expectation.
Ears cocked, tongue out, tail up, she waits
until you rise and follow her, come, like
Anubis, to lead you from the living. I hope
she led you well, Rafael, and I hope when you arrived
you could hear the music where I danced.

Ancestors

Photos in an old trunk.
All those faces no one recognizes.
Why should I care
that I will be forgotten?

Ballad to Lorca

"If only the sun were shining tonight..."
ANDRÉ BRETON

Antonio went down to the river, you wrote,
two lemons were day in his hands;
they, singing their smooth yellow songs
like two suns in his fingers' cage.
Canary-bright color the stream
when he threw the two lemons in:
alchemical toss of the hand
to turn a dark river to gold!

In Jerez de la Frontera,
your gypsies make suns at the forge.
Not hammering horseshoes or tools,
they shape only saffron and light.
At anvils, they fashion July,
make noon of night's iron and cold's tin.
The gypsies mold silver-scaled fish
into arching beams of the sun.

Your Almerían gypsy nun
is surrounding herself with gold;
five grapefruit sleep in her kitchen;
her windows are painting the light.
She embroiders straw-colored cloth
with needle and sunflowered thread
in order to weave her own sky,
in bloom, now, with twenty bright suns.

*   *   *

O Lorca, what is the darkness
they seek to destroy with their suns?
"The black bull with veins of silver—
the crescent-horned night that is Death,
the moon who makes marble of sleep,
the dream that intrudes upon day.
No noon can alter its coming,
and the fish that's dusk slips away."

Belchite

Here there was a room once painted blue:
you can see it on the bit of wall still standing.
There, tilts a steeple full of holes, no bells.
Beyond, a staircase rises into nothing. Piles of rubble
lie in heaps like arbitrary cairns.

This is Belchite, a humming, prosperous town in Aragon
'til Franco rose against Spain's new Republic.
The war he started came here the next year:
in August of '37; then again in March of '38.
Two different battles gripped & racked this town.

And now it has been left to stand in ruins.
You can walk down the main street—broken
walls on either side, smashed lintels—to the end
of town. Turn round then and you'll pass by the old church,
roofless now, vaults arced with bullet holes;
on its door, this spray-painted graffito:

Pueblo viejo
De Belchite
Ya no te rondan
Zagales
Ya no se
Oirán las jotas
Que cantaban
Nuestros padres

Old town of
Belchite
Young men roam around you
No longer
The jota-*tunes our parents*
Used to sing
You hear
No longer

Now only
bands of ants.
Now only
the high-voiced cicadas.

Sid's Story

for Sid Harris and Tom Entwistle

I.   The Lincolns stood in groups around the bar.
                                              Keller
    was telling of a battle,
    Pappas, of the time
                    he swam the Ebro underfire.
    Someone said Gandesa,
                     and you told your story then:
    a small
          flower opening at the field's edge.

II.   I didn't think I'd make it through the night.
    That was fifty years ago,
                    lying in a ditch
                          outside Gandesa,
    one leg shattered,
             and a bullet
    shouting in my arm.
    Our troops had gone,
               and Franco's
                  would be there at any moment.
    Do you know how dark it gets out in the country?

III. I saw three figures coming down the road.
     Black
          detached from black.
                               Who?
    Then it was clear:
              three women,
                    two
    in widow's black,
    and one young girl
          who said she would come back to me with food:
    Asunción,
        the opening of heaven.

IV. A long time lapsed.
               Asunción returned.
    All that passed between us I can't say;
    I'd lose consciousness
             and wake
                  to hear her singing.
    She cradled me
          like I was something precious.
    She
      was the one,
          my moon under the pines.

V.   A second moon,
                              dove's head,
                                        it was an egg
                                                  she proffered:
delirium's dark wind
                    shape-changed our supper,
                                        warped the Spanish clouds.
The water in my cup
                    came from her breast.
Below us,
          night-migrations shook the grove:
herds
     of tramping boots;
                         smashed branches;
                                        shadow-crowds.

VI. We held on for weeks that night.
                                   Franco's men
                                        passed through.
With light came the more lenient Italians:
Russo?, they asked me.
                         No, I said,
                                   Chicago.
Ah, Chicago! Al Capone!
They grinned at me,
                    made sounds like Tommy-guns,
                                        and spared my life,
sent me
          to jail instead.
But I never saw Asunción again.

VII. Throughout my life

                         I've relived that one night:
I sleep, fall through the darkness, wake up
in her arms.

                   She is singing low, in Spanish;

                                          I
am dying and am falling fast in love.

                             It's the last
night I will ever see her face;
the end comes soon.

                     And yet, these fifty years,
she's what's appeared

               when I've looked at the moon.

January, 1939

Spring hasn't come yet to the Pyrenees.
The harsh terrain is unrelieved by lupine;
no gentians now, no grass green with the sun,
no sun. Later, the white hawthorn,
but now snow. Rocky outcroppings, ice-
sheathed. Steep, slick road carved with cold.

Antonio Machado, old man of Spanish poetry,
trudges along the road that leads from Spain.
His mother, whom another refugee has dubbed "older
than God", walks wearily beside him.
The war is all but lost. Franco has crushed
the Republic, and the road streams with those
who've chosen exile, trying to reach the French frontier;
the Spaniards pour like blood from unstaunched wounds.

In the dimming light, Machado lifts his eyes
at the passing of a slow convoy of trucks.
Reading a label, he realizes:
the Prado Museum is traveling at his side.

*   *   *

The story usually stops here, its
denouement the strange coincidence
of the meeting of the poet and the paintings
on the hard road out of Spain.

But I like to take it further, imagining Machado
picturing to himself all that's inside: the lapis,
rose, and gold world of Angelico's annunciation,
where Mary receives the message
as if it is a warm wind blown through violets;
the quicksand-colored void overwhelming
the small head of Goya's drowning dog,
whose eyes show that it knows it won't be saved;
the barefoot spinner of Velázquez, turned
to her task, her white shoulder somehow
as radiant as another's face;
Titian's Danäe, pale, and waiting like the rest of us
for love to shower down its golden rain...

Everyone assumes Machado's grief
was sharpened by this sight of art in flight
—his heart failed him within a month—
and yet to have their company could have
seemed a momentary grace, a brief respite,
like the presence of a sweet-faced donkey
in a brutal painting of the crucifixion,
or even, in that same work, the deep
colors, the harmony of intersecting lines.

Royal Armory, Madrid

(Spring, 2003)

Here, helmets, silver breastplates, smooth
cuirasses. A metal horse's hood,
forged sabots, even a convex
stomach-plate (for a pot-bellied knight?).

The exhibits come chronologically:
chain-mail gives way to steel plates, and
armor becomes more extensive, until
every part has its covering—gorget, gauntlet, greave.
The metal suit is total, and even the horses
have caparisons of steel.

How brief was the time they felt invulnerable?
Armor's apex had been reached, the man-casing
complete. A moment maybe when the one inside it
believed he could do battle with impunity.
How long before gunpowder put a hole...?

Outside the Armory, young sailors on leave
loll in the late sunlight. Their caps all say
"Armada": no surprise, this is the Spanish Navy;
I'm the only one for whom they conjure 1588,
the invincible fleet sent out against the British.

Blossoms no more fragile than our flesh
drift in the breeze, land on the English
newspaper: "'U.S. War Machine
Unbeatable' Says Bush". The lesson still
unlearned. I set off, but fail to look
before I cross the streaming boulevard.

Café Ephemeral

Plum tree in full flower,
blossoms scattered by an early wind.

*   *   *

1927. Bright afternoon, Café Gijón, Madrid.
They've had to get more chairs, another table.
Alberti, Lorca, Cernuda, Salinas, Guillén
here together, planning a 300th birthday banquet
for Góngora, whose ancient complex forms
they seize and fill with modern images:
"Madrigal on a Tram Ticket"—Alberti pulls
his latest from his pocket. He reads,
they laugh, shout one more line, and Lorca
sings out a refrain. Something has cohered.
The air between them shimmering & fragrant.
Then, war. Soon exile, death.

1913. Midnight, the Stray Dog Cabaret, St. Petersburg.
The walls & ceiling bright with fantastical
birds, with flowers conjured by Baudelaire.
Blok's wife performs his poems there.
Akhmatova recites to Mandelstam; across
the room, declaiming a competing reading,
Mayakovsky with his drum, wearing a carrot,
and Khlebnikov, his poem-birds kept safe
inside a pillowcase. Later came Tsvetaeva.
Their voices all explode, entwine. Just
for this brief time. Then world war,
revolution, civil war, the purges, and the camps.
Only Akhmatova left, her early words now true:
"There's nobody left alive to hear what I say".

1908. Evening, Lapin Agile Café, Paris.
Here they'd dipped the donkey's tail
into red & yellow & blue, laid a canvas
on the floor, titled the work, "The Sun Goes Down
Over the Adriatic". Now, Guillaume Apollinaire
amidst a swirl of painters—Braque with his
accordion, Picasso: all the sides
of the cube at the same time! And poets—
Jacob, Salmon: words on a page not
chronological, but simultaneous, splashed
in circling patterns; a book on one long page
seen entire at a glance! Banquets, manifestoes,
Chinese lanterns. Everything at once, then
not at all. The war. A shellburst in his trench.
Apollinaire, trepanned, weak, died of the flu
during the last hours of the war; they were shouting
down the Kaiser in the boulevard below, "À bas
Guillaume!"; he thought they cried at *him*.

1911. Morning, a café in Schwabing, Munich.
A sharing of canvasses: Franz Marc paints paradisial
blue horses; Kandinsky's riders balance
on the edge of abstraction. Coalescence
of the Blue Rider Group: towards "a rebirth
of looking". August Macke, whose palette
pulses like a tropical aviary, helps them
put the Almanac together, "Every day here
is a party". Kandinsky's objects start
to melt; Marc's horses joined by sweet-
faced deer, by fox & dog & antelope, creatures
from another place, mysterious envoys bearing
the secret of tenderness. "Our movement will know

neither nationality nor frontiers, but only
humanity". Three summers later, war's declared.
Kandinsky's given one day to depart, "it was as if
I had been snatched out of a dream".
In September, Macke is killed, and later, at Verdun,
Franz Marc, and with him, all the reimagined
animals of Eden, exploded, falling, swallowed
by the earth, taking their secret with them.

                    *   *   *

Always the sun hurried into the sea,
the dazzling engulfed by the dark.

Soliloquy of a Herd-Watcher

The solitude of shepherds hangs in me
As heavy and as stiff as a cloth robe.
The bells, the wind, the bleating are one note.
Tonight has knit the noise: my sighs are songs.
My thoughts are as the stirring of the leaves;
My stories lie like ghosts among the coals.
The sleep of sheep breathes sadness in the grass
And makes me feel I must explain the stars.
Night's sorrow is a sound incapable
Of movement, a lost meaning in the dark.

The Duende* and the Muse Contend for the Heart of the Poet

The Muse: I shall ride through your mind on a zebra,
          patrolling the borders of black and of white,
          dividing the chess-pieces of language
          as the horizon divides the fish from the cloud.

The Duende: I'll pour burning oil on your delicacy's snow,
          throw cream on your black velvet sorrow!

The Muse: I shall be as a nest of blue robin's eggs
          in the elm at the base of your tongue.

The Duende: I'll be wind in the elm's leafless branches,
          I'll be lightning to hollow its trunk,
          I'll be thunder to make its roots quiver:
          I'll be storm to chase squirrels from your mouth.

The Muse: I shall cut opals out of the moon
          that you may wear them on the fingers
          of your song.

The Duende: I'll polish the moon with sandpaper
          and cause it to howl in answer
          to its coyote lover.

* The Duende is the dark, Dionysian opposite of the radiant, Apollinian Muse.
It is the name which the Andalusian Spanish give to the daemonic spirit of inspiration.

The Muse: I shall be the sound of the shadow of leaves.

The Duende: I'll be the leonine roar of the sun!

The Muse: I shall bathe your wrists
               with water from the Heliconian spring.

The Duende: I'll drown your ankles in the flame
               of red wine.

The Muse: I shall cause lilies
               to open in your sleep.

The Duende: I'll twist your dreams
               with the vines of climbing roses.

The Muse: I shall tint the afternoon with lupine
               and the dusk with violets.

The Duende: I'll paint the noon with ravens
               and surprise midnight with bluebirds.

The Muse: I shall teach you the grace of a feather.

The Duende: I'll teach you the anger of stone.

The Muse: I shall embroider your sleeves
             with immortality's lace.

The Duende: I'll hang Death's cape
             from your shoulders.

The Muse: I shall preside at conception;
             like morning glories your limbs
             shall I entwine.

The Duende: I'll preside at birth,
             causing your back
             to arch in a rainbow of pain,
             and the colors of hyacinth, jonquil, and iris
             shall burst your earthen body
             with Spring.

The Chinese Papercutter

The Chinese papercutter
fashions dragons with scissors

       or with a knife of moon:

              a fish fashioning water.

He dreams of cardinals
and finds his paper red—

       the shadow of a poinsettia wing
       on his design

              covering it
              as the appleskin's flame
              covers pale fruit.

He moves so slightly
it is as if he does not
move at all.

       Motionless roses thus
       arrange themselves
       in vases

              like hills
              which at last declare their outlines
              to the painter.

His is an art of patience,
devoid of disquietude:

he does not envy the silken kites
their intimacy with the wind

nor does he begrudge the flute
its ability to carve
melodies.

Sonnet to Chagall

Silver moon sliver swims in scarlet seas,
A fish, suspended, shines in smoother skies;
Women walk round with pictures on their knees
And great bouquets grow out of their green eyes.
What must your horse have been to conjure this:
Transparent mares whose striped wombs carry goats—
And could your wife have dreamt that her soft kiss
Would turn into the touch of wind on boats?
Your brush is no dull craftsman's stillborn tool
But Merlin's golden flicker of a wand,
Whose touch creates a circus from a rule
And, leaving logic, finds blue suns have dawned.
Your vision pleases more than it alarms;
Who doubts a pair of lovers has ten arms?

To Sinbad

My own landscape
is not like yours—
oceans where fish
fly with heads
like owls
and rivers run
with rubies—
yet my dreams
are as rich:
elk with tall, cool
candles in their antlers
light the summer
stars,
and turquoise falls
from the wings of
bright peacocks.
My eyes are as
uncharted
as your seas.
It is our directions
which divide us:
centripetal
and centrifugal,
the tendency
of petals
to turn inward,
the tendency
of fast music
to flee the score.

Maybe I Am Robert Burns' Descendant

Dumfriesshire, Scotland
April, late 1700's

I imagine you, the young wife
of my ancestor Kirkpatrick. Out walking,
with a basket on your arm. To market?
Except you strayed down to the river:
maybe a flare of color caught your eye—
wildflower on the bank—or maybe the Nith
was glimmering, the sun new after Winter.
And Burns had come there too, to see
the shining light that afternoon, but he saw *you*.
You knew who he was—you lived in the same county—
the poet & song catcher, with a dangerous
reputation as a lover of women.
But when he stopped to talk, you stayed
to listen, drawn in. And when he asked
to walk with you the next week, you agreed.

A leaf or a flower on the current, borne by it,
a gentle yet unstoppable force. Pulling. His voice
must have enchanted you, and the power
of his words: to what did he compare you?
Moonlight catching trout-gleam, the tender
pale, first petallings of Spring?
You must have found him irresistible.
Did you feel re-flowered by his touch?

The baby was assumed to be your husband's.
Years later, Robbie already dead, the child
became a singer. I wonder if you ever caught
that same seductive sparkling in his eyes?

Running with the Maenads

It was the Spring your father died
and you fell in love
and all you really wanted to do
was run with the Maenads
like the Greek women of old
all silently leaving their houses
when the moon was full
meeting at the edge of the woods
then taking off, running, each alone
but all surrounded by the others
screaming at first
then shouting with ecstasy and grief
each translating her story to a cry
continuing to run until their outstretched arms
—unworking wings cutting the night—
came finally to embrace the warm air
and they at last grew satiated, silent
dropping down under flowering boughs
to stare up at the white moon through white blossoms.

Two Visions

The trees in their redwood planters
are growing stunted.
We have carried them about
from rented house to house,
envisioning someday a planting
in a garden of our own:
roots finally put into the earth
and limbs unbending, stretched sunwards.

Seeing the stunted trees, whose leaves,
too small, have turned, again, too early,
I long for a piece of land that is our own:
a tree-home, a landscape
we'd come to know in every season
and at every time of day—
a place to witness growth;
there, we might even, like the ancient Scandinavians,
place a baby in the branches
of a newly planted tree,
in ceremonious token
of a decision to plant roots, and foster life
outside ourselves.

But then I think of islands,
green, in the Pacific,
and of the scent of unnamed flowers,
of walking by the shore alone, enrapt
—or sailing with a stranger—
the light sparkling on the sea,
and the wind heard always by the heart
as a plangent bell...

And I know then that I don't know
what I want—garden or voyage—
and, not knowing, may end
like an imaginary bird
whose instinct failed her, and
not knowing whether to migrate or to nest,
did neither, but remained upon her branch,
singing her uncertainty
to the fixed and moving stars.

Now
      it is Autumn.
No more green shoots.
Only regret flowers:
I think of you and wonder
If, last Spring, that seed
Had gone to ground...
Would I have cupped bright petals,
Found the bloom to be perennial?

The Sea of Cortez

I had never heard of it
when you first said you'd
take me there: the Sea
of Cortez, nebulous,
silvery, galleon-crossed.
Then I found it on a map,
and it came less to signify a time
than a place, a body
of water between Baja and Mexico.
An article you found described it:
blue bays, in which lay small
bare islands with cacti candelabra.

Aided thus, my imagination
formed another picture, but it was
so suffused with light, and with
your presence, with childhood
notions of voyages, and an adult's desire
for adventure and for change, that I knew
it was not a picture of a place.

Now that I am not coming with you after all,
the Sea of Cortez grows increasingly unreal.
It has faded back into silver, and
I see it now only in snatches: sparkles,
ripples, wings of lone birds, the kind of
synecdoche that takes place in dreams.
Soon, the Sea of Cortez will cease
to be a place, will be for me a name
for possibility, unrealized, unlit
by the sun, but shining, still, in the mind.

Letter to John

Dear John,
                The danger
lies in living—long before I reach her age—
in the manner of my grandmother:
the present a blur, un-
grasped, the days of her past
bright before her.
What do we do with our experience?

Remember: the zoo animals you
brought to life from sleeping stones?
the moonpath our eyes
shaped to a perfect curve?
the unlooked-for storm that broke
on the still lake & quiet mountain?
July moons are blotting out
my August suns.

I need to hear again
one of your lessons on seeing,
or perhaps, one of your stories—
your grandfather's, about the Cherokee
who took leave of the lake he loved
by paying homage to its four directions,
remembering his time in each; this tribute
enabled him to turn away…I imagine him
relinquishing the shining water, but am caught up
wondering: did he ever see that lake again?
Write me the ending, John.
                      Love,
                      Carolyn

Postcard from Lanikai

She doesn't say
             whether or not
the patch is taking on the marriage
(the real reason they're there in that far place)

writes only
that the Hawai'ian waters
                       soft to sink into, thickly salty, warm
are closing up the pierced holes in her ears

and that she's begun
                  to wear her ear-studs to the beach
in order to prevent their being healed.

The Right Hand and the Left

She is comfortable there, quiet
among the quiet blue of things:
sleeping china, paintings into whose
dreams she freely enters.
                But it was good that day
                she let inside the Mardi Gras parade,
                like letting in a wind all full of birds—
                bright feathers, noisy music—
                and when they left she thought
                of leaving with them.

She is well-loved at home, feels
devotion as she feels the sun
warming her whole body when,
after swimming, she climbs up on the hot
rocks and bathes in the soft air.
                And yet she seeks the company of strangers,
                enduring the cold & the storm
                just for that rare flash of lightning,
                the open place in the sky afterwards.

In her house she feels as solid
as her house, no cracks, a
smooth sculpture, complete.
　　　　　　　Between sleeping & waking, though,
　　　　　　　she feels the fissures opening inside her,
　　　　　　　glimpses a gleam like gems (a cave
　　　　　　　of jewels, or just a superficial
　　　　　　　shine?) and knows then that she's dying
　　　　　　　to be mined.

The Form of Loss

A cabin in Switzerland:
we sit across the table from each other.

I see it clearly as I read your letter:
wooden table, wooden benches,
the dining room of some small inn;
firelight, and dusk's rose-light through a window;
we're laughing at something one of us has said.

The trouble is, we've never been
to Switzerland (we've known each other
such a little while), and what the letter's saying
is goodbye.

I can't think why my loss should take this form
—a picture of a time we never shared—
and wonder at the image
'til I see it is an emblem
of the future we won't have, a reminder

that we could have found ourselves
in sudden sunlight at the margin of some meadow,

climbed the flowered hills all afternoon,
and ended, in the evening, at a cabin in the mountains,
seated across a table from each other.

Wedding Poem

When your face
appeared over my life
        the smallest sun:
                love's only one luminous point,
                yet it takes over all of time,
                spreading its light over all that came before it,
                and all that will come after

at first I understood
only the poverty of what I have
        as the ground would understand
        the sparseness of spring snow
           the white of my gown
           a Saxon symbol
           that I come to you
           with nothing.

Then its particular light
on woods, on rivers, on the sea,
        the way the wind
        changes the green of the fields
           the blowing roses of Carcassonne:
           a dichotomy of petal and shadow

became my beginning in the colored world
in which I had not yet had my beginning
                    it is said that
                    birds are blind
                    to the color blue
                              my world, hitherto
                              a bird's sky

...the flower I was waiting for,
the blue flower, the rose
of my echoing country
                         you are the larkspur
                         and the lupine,
                                   the luminous poppy
                                   of night's orchard.

I am of an old race of darkness and forests,
but while I bend down as in a well and enter
feeling my way like a blind man in my own territory,
I find no railing to direct my steps,
but, instead, the growth of your rose in my own dwelling...
                    a Braille of bloom
                              a silver banister of song
                              down the throat's stairway.

...So, here...we live
like a single plant which cannot explain its leaves
>> the enchanted Vine
>> now one with the Castle
>>> an infusion of the sky with the dawn:
>>> a lily on the back of a swan.

Perhaps very late
our dreams joined
at the top or at the bottom,
up above like branches moved by a common wind,
down below like red roots that touch
>> Philemon and Baucis join in spite of bark's impasse,
>> weave an arras of changing shadows on the grass
>>> even as I weave verses that I might wed:
>>> *I touch only the heart of things*
>>> *now I hold the thread.*

white blossoms like rice
i am the bride of spring wind
petals in my hair

Curing the Drought

This year, the plum blossoms are drying as they bud.
Spring, but the streams aren't running, the hills
already brown. The wind feels ominous
over the fields, and certain birds
are not even building their nests. All of nature
seems uneasy, out of joint, unsure.
Give me your mouth, love, and kiss my parched lips.
Let our kisses rain down on the world, o let them
green the fields, restore the salmon to full streams,
fill the air with those rare butterflies
that can't mate against blue sky.

April in Vermont:
in bare trees the birds, just back,
substitute for leaves.

In Vermont

It is melting season here.
April, and suddenly the still
landscape is loud with voices. Not just
those of the birds, newly returned,
but water-voices: everywhere the sun
is melting ice & snow, and rivulets,
streams, waterfalls are pouring,
coursing, rushing down the mountainside.
Listen: what was mute as cloud
now sings the jostling songs of glass.
It is the tale where White Buffalo
dissolves into a chant of rain.
But what if this transformation—silent, solid
white into voiced transparency—
took over the whole countryside? What if
the birches, too, should melt
and begin ringing out like bells?

Parrots

They sit up in the trees like Dadaists—
Tzara & Breton perched with tipped pails
waiting to surprise evening commuters.

Each has escaped confinement, squeezed
through an open window, found the others.
Wild now, and free, they've formed a company.

You can see them above Berkeley, one low
fast-moving cloud green as March grass,
close-gathered flock of newly uncurled leaves.

But every day at five they head for BART,
settle in the trees outside the station, and yell
"I love you!" & "Hi, there!" to all who pass.

The people like their greeters, like
the interruption of their thoughts,
the intrusion of the bright unusual;

and always, there is someone
hearing them for the first time:
she's the one you see turning around,

wondering for a second if the words
are meant for her, then smiling
as she realizes who spoke them.

But it's the birds I mainly think about.
Parrots love pranks, of course, and maybe
these miss practicing their English.

Still I wonder why they come.
What memory of a head turned,
sudden as a falling star, or a voice

speaking a name barely remembered,
draws each one here
to call out 'til the night arrives, and

they ascend in a swirl of green dotted with gold,
bouquet of speaking acacia
offered to the quiet darkening sky.

In My Father's Garden

The unusual blue hyacinth came into bloom
unnoticed, and now the apple tree surprises me:
already in full flower.
The daffodils he planted here last fall
have all come up, bright gold in the March dusk.
He has had to leave his home, go
elsewhere to be cared for, and I've
come back here to look in on his garden.
Does the camellia care there's no face at the window?
Do the birds in the branches miss the one who watched them?
Does it matter to the tulips that they opened up, then
faded, unappreciated and unseen?
For fifty years, his eyes admired this garden, every flower;
I might expect to find their imprint on these petals.

Le Rayon Vert

The day had been already blessed:
you had seen whales—their spouts
& arcing tails, white
puffs & glittering black way out to sea.
Then just as the sun set: a peal
of color, the green ray, an emerald
flash, light leaping
out of beryl newly opened.
                          A green shout. Cézanne's green. Voice
                          of willows darkening the deep
                          green of a pond, voice of the tips
                          of firs, uncurling April leaves,
                          a mallard's head, new
                          grass, a dragonfly.

You'd heard of it before—
from Coleridge, Jean Rhys, and
that film *Le Rayon Vert* in which
the heroine, whose life's a mess,
wanders the world and winds up
one evening on a far beach in Brazil.
She sees the *rayon vert*: her shut
accordion-life swings wide again.
                          A green release of birds.

And *your* life? Another instance
of the world speaking to you,
its searchlight finding you,
its traffic light now finally
saying "Go!"
An Annunciation, but instead
of a golden ray from heaven,
this streamed from *earth*'s horizon,
and was green.

                    Unencumbered by angelic mediation,
                    you are free to make your own translation.
                    Say good news.

Santorini

The swallows still swoop
                and
                      plunge
when dusk begins to soften the bright air.
Little now remains of what was here—
where a mountain rose, a blue caldera shines,
brimming with the Mediterranean sea—but the swallows
still etch wild arabesques above the island.

Just so, you can see them, streaking across
the side of a clay pot from Akrotiri,
and free-falling in the wall-paintings made
four thousand years ago when this was Thira.

Birds, animals, and flowers animate
the Thiran frescoes: climbing monkeys painted
vivid blue; red lilies swaying; playing
antelopes; careening swallows. Sometimes, too,
a boy or girl or goddess in the foreground.
One of these last is named by the museum plaque
"The Mistress of the Animals".

On the painting's left, a young girl offers saffron.
On the right, the receiving goddess sits.
A beauty, herself, she is arrayed in beauty.
Tall, with arresting eyes and long, curling hair—
a living snake for headband—she wears
a flowing skirt that falls in colored flounces,
a finely decorated shawl, delicate loop earrings, deep
blue bracelets, and a three-tiered necklace of rose
beads, tiny carved ducks, gold dragonflies.
Beside the goddess hovers a mythical beast,

the winged griffon. But between the goddess and the girl,
an actual animal stands, an upright monkey.
The plaque says he's an intermediary:
because animals are closer to nature, it explains,
this culture deemed them nearer the divine.

A different hierarchy of being!
Quick as the thought, a pouring out of animals.
Unnetted dolphins leap; across the ocean,
bears rush out of hiding, float above the salmon.
Unpoisoned wolves walk into pools of light,
unbeaten harp seals glimmer at the edges of the ice.
Unbeached by sonar, whales each complete
the fourteenth variation on their song.
The buffalo come back, the butterflies who
lost their habitats now flash their wings...

O, more dazzling than her jewelry!

The swallows swirl a living crown
above the little that remains.

Animal Dreams

Sleeping spaniel, what are you dreaming of? Everyone
says squirrels, but maybe
it's a different realm entirely, lilac-
suffused: I've seen the purple
of your gaze when I've just waked you.

At least you don't dream of standing
before your class without your clothes on,
of losing your luggage in a railway station—
the self's banal anxieties about its presentation to the world.

Let's say you dream into being
some of the texture of this world; let's say
we need your dreams. Let's say the liquid
sound we love—cottonwood leaves in the wind—
is linked to some parched bird dreaming of water.

Why have we rid the world of fairies,
dryads, naiads, brownies, elves? Milton
says Christ's crying in his infancy
drove the deities & demi-deities away.
And now we're driving out sea-turtles, monarch butterflies,
species of pines & lilies, wolves & foxes, diving birds.
The world will be less rich without their presence—but what about
their dreams? What if they've all been partly dreaming
us, and lacking them, our world becomes
as trivial and narrow as our dreams?

Moonnight Considers Argos

People all think Odysseus
had it hard, but it was his dog
who got the short end of the stick.
Odysseus faced six-headed Scylla,
Circe, the Sirens, the Whirlpool,
the giant looming Cyclops who ate men.
He sailed even to the mouth
of Hades, forced endlessly to roam.
But Argos sat by the door
for twenty years, and waited
for his master to come home.

Wishbone for the Millennium

(after a sketch by Deianna Greet, 1999)

I cannot make out what you've drawn this time:
a giant floating wishbone
                                eyed with three setting suns?
It conjures a wish for the new Millennium.

Useless, to wish the end of war, cruelty, disease
(although I wish the end of all of these).
Useless to wish
                        for the lessening of loss,
or the diminishment of pain.

And so I wish
                    for a continued sense
of abundance on the periphery:
forests that stretch
                        beyond what we can see
off to either side of the highway;
spoor of mountain-lion on the trail;
evidence of eagles. It doesn't matter
that we see them, only that we know
they're there, that there exists
                                a multiplicity of life
just outside the range of our perception,
always a glimmer at the edge of vision,
like the gleam of phosphorescence
                                off the boat's wake,
proclaiming
fish as many as stars.

What a comfort
                    to think there might remain
unharvested hives of honey, fields of wild
                                        lavender
that never finds its way to any vase,
birdsong untaped, useless wild things
                                        existing for themselves,
whose presence, nonetheless,
gives a shine to our lives,
                    the way
those cracked stones carried far up on the bank
quicken
            with reflected light from off the river.

Lapidary

Albertus Magnus tells the virtues
of the stones: take *gerachidem*, he says,
let one hold it in his mouth;
it maketh him that bears it merry.
If borne before the heart, *hephaestites*
makes a man sure. Albertus tells us
where to find these stones: in the nest
of a black plover; in the belly of a swallow; in
seawater, where the waves break off the shore.
And some must be specially bound: with red thread
to the wing of an owl; to a wolf's tooth & a laurel leaf.

And to cure the ache of a lost friendship?
Shall I take a faded stone,
wrap it in a letter from that friend,
pulverize it, mix the dust with seeds
of native flowers, scatter in the garden?
Or for help accepting mutability? Why not
make a necklace of a worn beach pebble
whose surface, wet when you find it,
reflects a bit of passing cloud.
To ward off the hour's thinness,
take a variegated stone found in a pool
where trout flash in the depths;
place it in the heart of a flower
blooming entirely hidden by its leaves.

But what if the stone—any stone—
feels too heavy, and delight
lies only in turning it to a warm wind?
The lifting of the heron's what you need,
a shape-shift to something lighter.
Choose the running stream over the lake;
observe smoke as it rises.
Not even the peach blossom, but its fragrance.

Note on "Wedding Poem"

This poem is, in part, a *cento*. The lines in italics are "samplings" from other poets; weaving their lines in with my own enabled me to have them in attendance at my wedding.

The poem is composed of eight stanzas, each having three tiers.

—The first two lines of each of the first four stanzas are from "Colours" by Yevgeny Yevtushenko, translated by Robin Milner-Gulland and Peter Levi. Reprinted by permission of Penguin Random House U.K.

—The fourth through seventh lines of the first stanza are my translation from the French of a passage from *Adolphe* by Benjamin Constant.

—The first three lines of the fifth stanza are from "Your Laughter" by Pablo Neruda, from THE CAPTAIN'S VERSES, copyright 1972 by Pablo Neruda and Donald D. Walsh. Reprinted by permission of New Directions Publishing Corp.

—The first five lines of the sixth stanza and the first two lines of the seventh stanza are from "Serenade" by Pablo Neruda, translated by Kenneth Rexroth, and published by City Lights Books. Reprinted by permission of the Kenneth Rexroth Trust.

—The first five lines of the final stanza are from "Night on the Island" by Pablo Neruda from THE CAPTAIN'S VERSES, copyright 1972 by Pablo Neruda and Donald D. Walsh. Reprinted by permission of New Directions Publishing Corp.

—The final two lines are from "Vigilance" by André Breton, translated by Kenneth White.

Acknowledgments

Grateful acknowledgement is made to the following periodicals, in whose pages these poems first appeared.

ATLANTA REVIEW: "The Poet of Poet Laval"

BLUE UNICORN: "Lapidary," "The Next Poem," and "The Sea of Cortez"

CALIFORNIA STATE POETRY QUARTERLY: "Ballad to Lorca," "Sonnet to Chagall," and "The Chinese Papercutter"

CHAMINADE LITERARY REVIEW: "Now it is Autumn...," "Postcard from Lanikai," and "Two Visions"

CHOWDER REVIEW: STANFORD UNIVERSITY: "To Sinbad"

KAIMANA: LITERARY ARTS HAWAI'I: "Withdrawal and Return"

MAGAZINE: "Le Rayon Vert"

REDWOOD COAST REVIEW: "Anubis," "Parrots," and "In My Father's Garden"

SANSKRIT:"The Duende and the Muse Contend for the Heart of the Poet"

WHISPERING CAMPAIGN: "In Vermont"

The author also wishes to acknowledge and thank the Vermont Studio Center and the Leighton Studios at the Banff Centre, where some of these poems were written.

~

Thank you to Ann May and to Holly Schmidt for their enduring friendship, and their encouragement over the years. And thanks to Ann, too, for her help with the cover.

Thank you to Shay Black, Tim Dunlap, Roger Greenwald, and John Kottcamp for the special inspiration each has given me.

Deep gratitude to my friends and fellow writers Stephen Kessler and Marta Maretich for the examples of excellence they have set me, for the literary camaraderie we have shared, for their helpful and insightful comments, and for their belief in this work.

Thanks, too, to the many members of the American Literary Translators Association—gifted writers all—for their interest in, and support of, my original work.

Thank you to the artist Deianna Greet for our collaboration, and for the sketches that inspired some of these poems.

Thank you to my brother, the writer James G. Tipton, for the joy we've had in exchanging poems and editorial suggestions over so many years.

Thank you to all my dogs through time—Leaf, Moonnight, Tristan, and Olé—for their steady, quiet companionship.

A bouquet of gratitude to Jessie Lendennie and Siobhán Hutson at Salmon Poetry for bringing this book into the world.

Thank you always to my husband, Frank Kucera, for his perennially unwavering generosity, understanding, and appreciation.

Photo: Wendy Leyden

CAROLYN L. TIPTON, born and raised in Berkeley, California, is a poet, translator, and teacher. She has a Master's Degree in English/Creative Writing from Stanford University and a B.A., M.A., and Ph.D. in Comparative Literature from the University of California, Berkeley, where she currently teaches in the Fall Program for Freshmen. She has published many poems and translations both in various journals, including *Partisan Review* and *Two Lines*, and in anthologies, including *Norton's World Poetry: An Anthology of Verse from Antiquity to Our Time,* and Robert Hass' *Now and Then: The Poet's Choice Columns, 1997-2000.* She has been the recipient of various grants and awards, including fellowships from the National Endowment for the Humanities and the National Endowment for the Arts. She has also been awarded writing residencies at The Banff Centre and the Vermont Studio Center. She has given readings of her poems and translations in the U.S., Mexico, Canada, and Spain. Her first book of translations of the poetry of Alberti, *To Painting: Poems by Rafael Alberti* (Northwestern University Press), won the National Translation Award. Her second, *Returnings: Poems of Love and Distance* (White Pine Press) won the Cliff Becker Translation Prize.

salmonpoetry
Cliffs of Moher, County Clare, Ireland

"Like the sea-run Steelhead salmon that
thrashes upstream to its spawning ground,
then instead of dying, returns to the sea –
Salmon Poetry Press brings precious cargo
to both Ireland and America in the poetry
it publishes, then carries that select work to
its readership against incalculable odds."

TESS GALLAGHER

The Salmon Bookshop & Literary Centre

Ennistymon, County Clare, Ireland

Listed in *The Irish Times'* 35 Best Independent Bookshops